Contents

Introduction

'It seems to me that love is everywhere. It isn't big news – but it's always there. Fathers and sons, mothers and daughters, husbands and wives, friends and strangers. ... If you look for it, you'll find – I think – that love actually is all around us ...'

It is not long before Christmas – a time for families, a time for love.

Peter and Juliet are getting married, but not everyone is so happy. Jamie loses his girlfriend. Mark is in love with a girl who will never be his. Sarah's love for her brother makes it difficult for her to find a boyfriend. Harry's love for his wife, Karen, is going to be tested by a beautiful new employee. Daniel's wife has just died. Billy Mack, the ageing rock star, is alone after a lifetime of singing about love. And the new British Prime Minister is a very lonely man.

So is love really all around us? Can these people find it? Is there enough magic in the world for everyone, even at Christmas?

The film *Love Actually* (2003) stars Hugh Grant as the Prime Minister, Alan Rickman as Harry, Emma Thompson as Karen, Colin Firth as Jamie, Liam Neeson as Daniel, and many other famous British actors. It was written by Richard Curtis, who has also worked on other very successful films like *Bridget Jones's Diary* (2001), *Notting Hill* (1999), *Bean* (1997) and *Four Weddings and a Funeral* (1994).

Chapter 1   Love Is All Around Us

'Whenever I feel unhappy about the state of the world,' the Prime Minister thought to himself, 'I think about the Arrivals gate at Heathrow Airport, where happy, smiling passengers greet their friends and relatives. It seems to me that love is everywhere. It isn't big news – but it's always there. Fathers and sons, mothers and daughters, husbands and wives, friends and strangers. When the planes hit New York, people's last phone calls weren't messages of hate. They were messages of love. If you look for it, you'll find – I think – that love actually is all around us ...'

♦

In a recording studio in London, an ageing rock star was recording a new song.

'I feel it in my fingers,
I feel it in my toes.'

Three much younger singers joined in enthusiastically:

'Love is all around me – and so the ...'

'I'm afraid you did it again, Billy!' his manager, Joe, called out.

'I know the old words so well.'

'We all do – and that's why we're doing these new ones.'

'Right. OK. Let's do it again.'

The music started again. Billy sang:

'I feel it in my fingers,
I feel it in my toes.
Love is all ... Oh no!'

The music stopped and then started again.

'I feel it in my fingers,
I feel it in my toes.
Christmas is all around me ...'

Joe smiled.

'And so the feeling grows.
It's written in the wind,
It's everywhere I go.
So if you really love Christmas
Come on and let it snow ...'

Billy stopped singing. 'This is rubbish, isn't it?' he said.

'Yes — complete rubbish, great rock star!' Joe agreed happily.

◆

In another part of the city, Jamie was preparing to go out. His girlfriend Katya watched him from the bed.

'I'm going to be late for the wedding,' he said anxiously.

'It's just round the corner. You'll be there in time.'

'You really don't mind me going without you?' he asked.

'No — I'm just feeling bad.'

'I love you,' Jamie told her, and he kissed her.

'I know.'

'I love you even when you're ill and look terrible.'

'I know. Now go, or you'll miss it.'

'Right.'

Jamie left the room, then put his head round the door again. 'Did I tell you that I love you?'

'Yes, you did,' Katya said impatiently. 'Now go!'

◆

A few streets away, Daniel sat alone in his home office, thinking about the recent death of his wife. He rested his head in his hands for a moment. Then he lifted his head, picked up the phone and rang his friend Karen.

'Karen — it's me again. I'm sorry. There's really nobody else I can talk to.'

Karen was in her kitchen, cooking her children's dinner. 'Of course we can talk,' she said. 'It's a bad moment now, though. Can I call you back in a minute?'

'Of course,' Daniel replied.

'It doesn't mean I'm not terribly sad that your wife just died.'

'Understood. Ring me later.' Daniel put the phone down.

Karen turned back to her seven-year-old daughter, Daisy. 'So — what's this big news?' she asked.

'We've been given our parts in the Christmas play,' Daisy told her. 'I'm the lobster.'

'The lobster?' said Karen.

'Yes.'

'In the Christmas play?'

'Yes,' said Daisy. 'First lobster.'

'There was more than one lobster at the birth of Jesus?'

'Yes!'

◆

In a church by a river, Peter was standing with his best man, Mark. It was his wedding day.

'No surprises?' Peter asked.

'No surprises,' Mark promised.

'Not like the stag night?'

'Unlike the stag night.'

'Those Brazilian women were a mistake, weren't they?'

'They were. Especially because they were actually men.'

'That's true. Good luck.'

They shook hands.

As the music started, Peter stepped forward and turned towards the back of the church. And there, walking towards him, was Juliet, smiling happily in her white wedding dress.

Mark picked up his video recorder and started to film.

Juliet walked more quickly until she was standing next to Peter. The service began. Wedding music played, songs were sung, and at the end of the service Peter and Juliet exchanged rings. The vicar smiled.

'You are now man and wife,' he told them, and the happy couple kissed.

Peter turned to Mark. 'No surprises. Good,' he said.

'No, I've grown up,' Mark replied.

At that moment, the traditional wedding music stopped, and from behind a curtain voices began to sing a Beatles song.

The curtain went back. Twenty people were singing 'All You Need Is Love'.

Juliet looked happily at Peter. 'Did you do this?'

'Er … No.' Peter looked at Mark. Mark looked away.

All around the church, people stood up and started joining in with their instruments. At the front, an electric guitarist appeared.

◆

On the same day the new Prime Minister's car, protected by police cars, drove along Downing Street and stopped outside number 10. There were crowds outside the building shouting his name. Journalists from TV, radio and the newspapers pushed forward with their microphones and cameras. The Prime Minister was a popular and attractive man.

Inside 10 Downing Street it was suddenly quiet after all the noise outside. The Prime Minister's personal adviser was waiting for him.

'Welcome, Prime Minister,' Annie said.

'I must practise my wave,' replied the Prime Minister. He kissed her.

'How are you feeling?' Annie asked.

'Good. Powerful.'

'Would you like to meet the people who work here?'

'Yes, very much, if that means I don't have to start running the country yet.'

Annie led him to a long line of employees. 'This is Terence, sir,' she said. 'He's in charge.'

'Good morning, sir,' Terence said.

'Good morning,' the Prime Minister answered. 'I had an uncle called Terence. I hated him. There was something very strange about him. I like the look of you, though.'

'This is Pat,' Annie said quickly.

'Good morning, sir. I'm responsible for arrangements in your private flat,' said Pat.

'Good morning, Pat. I'll be easier to look after than the last Prime Minister – no baby, no teenagers, no frightening wife.'

'And this is Natalie,' Annie said. 'She's new, like you.'

'Hello, Natalie,' said the Prime Minister.

'Hello, David – I mean, sir. Oh, I can't believe I said that. I'm so sorry, sir.'

'That's fine,' said the Prime Minister. He laughed as Natalie's face went prettily pink. Then he looked at her more carefully.

'Right,' said Annie. 'Let's fix the country, shall we?'

'Good idea! Why not?'

As the Prime Minister walked away, he looked back over his shoulder and took another quick look at Natalie. Then he went into his office.

'Oh no,' he said to himself. 'How inconvenient.'

Chapter 2   Alone and Sad

Back from Peter and Juliet's wedding, Jamie unlocked his front door and hurried into his living room. Another, slightly younger man came into the room at the same time from the kitchen.

'Hello!' Jamie said to his brother with surprise. 'What are you doing here?'

'Oh, I came round to borrow some old CDs,' Chris replied.

'Did the lady of the house let you in?'

'Yes.'

'Lovely, helpful girl. I came back before the reception to see if she was feeling better,' Jamie said. 'Listen, perhaps we should take Mum out for her birthday on Friday. What do you think? I feel we've been bad sons this year.'

'OK,' Chris agreed. 'That sounds fine – boring, but fine.'

Katya's voice came from the bedroom. 'Are you coming back to bed, darling? Jamie will be home soon.'

♦

By now, on the same beautiful winter day, Daniel and his eleven-year-old stepson were at his wife's funeral. A crowd of about eighty people filled the church, all dressed in black.

'And now,' said the vicar, 'Daniel wishes to say a few words.'

Daniel stood up and faced the guests. Behind him was a large picture of his wife, as she was before she died.

'Jo and I had a lot of time to prepare for this moment,' he began. 'Some of her requests were not very serious – I have not, for example, brought Claudia Schiffer with me to the funeral.' Even the vicar smiled. 'But she was quite clear about other things that she wanted. My darling girl, and Sam's darling mum, wanted to say her last goodbye to you, not through me but through the words of the great, the wonderful, Bay City Rollers.'

The Bay City Rollers were a pop group who were popular with young teenagers in the 1970s. Their terrible song, 'Bye Bye Baby', played loudly through the church.

And as the song played, more pictures were shown, including a twelve-year-old Jo dressed in a Bay City Rollers T-shirt.

The guests smiled at the song and the pictures, while their faces showed their deep sadness.

♦

6

That night, at Peter and Juliet's wedding reception, the guests were dancing. Mark was still filming.

Sarah, a friend whose phone never stopped ringing, sat down next to him and watched him with interest for a few minutes before she spoke.

'Do you love him?' she asked softly.

'Who? What?'

'Peter. Do you love him? I just thought I'd ask the question because it might be the right question. I mean, you might need to talk to someone and perhaps no one has ever asked you, so you couldn't talk about it ...'

'No, no, no is the answer. No. No!'

'So that's "no", is it?'

'Yes. Er ... this DJ – what do you think? Is he the worst DJ in history?'

'Probably,' Sarah replied. 'We'll know definitely when he plays his next song.'

The DJ looked out at the wedding guests. 'And here's one for lovers,' he said. 'Quite a lot of you are lovers, I expect ...'

He played the beginning of a very well-known and completely unsuitable song.

'Well, now we know,' said Mark.

'The worst DJ in the world,' Sarah agreed. 'No doubt.'

◆

The next day, Sarah was back at work in the large, untidy offices of Fairtrade, a company which bought from poor countries at fair prices.

A beautiful girl at the next desk got up and knocked on the door behind her.

'Come in,' said Harry.

Mia walked into Harry's office and smiled as her boss looked up. 'Sarah's waiting for you,' she said.

7

'Oh yes – of course. Good, good. Are you enjoying working here? Do you know whose advice not to listen to?'

'I think so.'

Mia left as Sarah came in.

'Hi, Harry.'

'Switch off your phone,' Harry said. 'Then tell me exactly how long you've been working here.'

'Two years, seven months, three days. And I think … about … two hours.'

'And how long have you been in love with Karl, our mysterious chief designer?' her boss asked.

Sarah looked surprised. 'Er …' she began, 'two years, seven months, three days and … about an hour and a half.'

'I thought so.'

'Do you think everybody knows?'

'Yes.'

'Do you think Karl knows?'

'Yes.'

'Oh, that is bad news.'

'And I was just thinking,' Harry continued, 'that maybe it's time to do something about it.'

'Like what?'

'Invite him out for a drink. Then, after about twenty minutes, say something like, "I would like to marry you and have your babies."'

'You know that?'

'Yes. And Karl does too. It would be best for all of us, I think. It's nearly Christmas.'

'Certainly – excellent. I'll do that. Thanks, boss.'

She opened the door to leave, and a very good-looking man walked in.

'Hi, Sarah,' Karl said.

'Hi, Karl,' Sarah replied.

Outside Harry's office, she stopped and took a deep breath. She switched on her phone and it rang immediately.

'Darling,' she said. 'Of course. Tell me.' She turned to Mia. 'Could you turn the music down? What is that song?'

It was 'Christmas Is All Around', by the ageing rock star Billy Mack.

◆

At a local radio station in Watford, on the edge of London, a DJ was playing Billy's new record. As it came to an end, the DJ spoke to his listeners.

'And that was the Christmas song by Billy Mack, who used to be a great musician. Has there been a worse song this century? I don't think so.' The DJ looked up and saw a second DJ waving at him. Looking down at the list of guests in front of him, he realized his mistake. 'And … yes … I believe Billy is a guest on my friend Mike's show in a few minutes. Welcome back, Billy.'

Billy and Joe were waiting outside the studio. The programme was playing in the room and they didn't look very happy. But ten minutes later, Billy was in the studio with DJ Mike.

'So, Billy, welcome back to radio. And your new Christmas song is "Love Is All Around".'

'Yes, but we've changed the word "love" to "Christmas".'

'Yes,' said Mike. 'Is that an important message for you, Billy?'

'No, not really, Mike. Christmas is for people who can share it with someone they love.'

'And that's not you?'

'That's not me. When I was young and successful, Mike, I was greedy and foolish. And now I'm grey-haired and alone.'

'Wow! Thanks for that, Billy.'

'For what?'

'For actually giving a real answer to a question. That doesn't often happen here at Radio Watford.'

'Ask me anything you like,' Billy said. 'I'll give you an honest answer.'

'OK, here's one – how do you think the new record compares to your old stuff?'

'Oh, Mike, you know as well as I do that the record's rubbish.' In the next room, Joe looked very unhappy. 'But wouldn't it be great,' Billy continued, 'if the Number One record in the charts this Christmas wasn't by a spotty teenager? Wouldn't it be great if it was by an old fool looking for new success at any price? All those young teenage stars will be in a hotel bedroom on Christmas Day with a good-looking girl. And I'll be in a cheap flat with my manager, Joe, the ugliest man in the world, feeling very unhappy because our idea for a Christmas song failed. So if you believe in Father Christmas, children – like your Uncle Billy – buy my Christmas song. And enjoy the line that's too long for the music …'

'I think you mean, "If you really love Christmas …" '

' "… Come on and let it snow." Yes, horrible!'

'So here it is one more time,' Mike said into his microphone for the listeners. 'A possible Christmas Number One – "Christmas Is All Around". Thank you, Billy. After this, the news. Is the new Prime Minister in trouble already?'

Billy went outside to Joe, smiling.

Chapter 3   Love Hurts

In Downing Street, a few days later, the Prime Minister and his ministers sat around a long table.

'OK,' the Prime Minister said. 'What's next?'

One of his ministers spoke. 'The American President's visit,' Carter told him.

'Ah, yes, yes. I'm worried about that.'

'There's a very strong feeling in the party, and in the country too, that we must be more independent than the last government was.'

'I agree,' said another minister. 'This is our first really important test. We must show the President that we don't take orders from him.'

'Right. Right. I understand that. But I have decided ... not to,' the Prime Minister told them. 'Not this time. We'll try to be clever, of course. But let's not forget, the US is the most powerful country in the world. I'm not going to start a fight that I can't win.' The ministers accepted this unenthusiastically. 'Right,' continued the Prime Minister. 'Now, how do I get a cup of tea and a biscuit in this place?'

At that moment Natalie came in with tea and biscuits. The Prime Minister's face turned red as she smiled at him.

'Good,' he said.

Later that day, there was a knock on the door of the Prime Minister's private office.

'Come in,' he called.

Natalie entered, carrying some files in one hand and a cup of tea and a plate of biscuits in the other.

'These have just arrived for you,' she said, giving the files to the Prime Minister. 'And this is for you too.'

The Prime Minister smiled. 'Excellent. Thanks.'

'I hoped you'd win,' Natalie continued. 'Although of course the other man would get biscuits, too, if he was here. But he wouldn't get *chocolate* biscuits.'

'Thank you very much, Natalie,' said the Prime Minister.

After she left, he lowered his head and hit it against the table top. 'Be sensible!' he said quietly to himself. 'You're the Prime Minister!'

◆

At Fairtrade, Harry and Mia were discussing the Christmas party.

'Not my favourite night of the year,' Harry said, trying not to stare at Mia's tight black dress. 'And it's your unhappy job to organise it.'

'Tell me.'

'Easy, really,' Harry said. 'Find a place for the party. Buy more drinks than anybody wants. Buy little things to eat – hundreds of them. And advise the girls not to go near Kevin.'

'Fine,' said Mia. 'Are we inviting wives and families?'

'Yes,' said Harry. 'I mean, not children – but husbands, wives, girlfriends ... You haven't got a horrible two-metre, tight-T-shirt-wearing boyfriend that you want to bring, have you?'

'No, I'll just wait under the mistletoe, hoping for a kiss.'

Their eyes met and an electric look passed between them.

'Right,' said Harry.

As Mia walked out, Harry shook his head like a man waking from a dream.

◆

Daniel was telling his friend Karen his worries about his stepson.

'Sam spends all his time in his room,' Daniel said. 'He's probably there now.'

'There's nothing unusual about that,' Karen told him. 'My horrible son Bernie stays in his room all the time. And I'm glad he does.'

'But this is *all* the time. And I'm afraid that there's something really wrong. I mean, he's sad about his mum, but he could be doing *anything* up there. If he was drinking beer and bringing women in, I wouldn't know.'

'At the age of eleven?'

'Well, maybe not women. Maybe just beer. The problem is, his mum always used to talk to him, and now the whole stepfather thing suddenly seems important. It wasn't before.'

'It's not surprising that this is a really horrible time. Just be patient – and maybe check his room for empty bottles.'

'And sometimes when he comes out of his room, I know he's been crying.' Tears suddenly ran down Daniel's face. 'It was such a waste when Jo died. And it's going to ruin Sam's life as well. I don't know what to do.'

Karen touched his shoulder. 'Be strong! People hate men who behave like girls. No one will ever want to spend time with you if you cry all the time.'

'You're right.'

That evening Daniel and Sam sat together, looking out across the River Thames.

Daniel took a deep breath. 'So what's the problem, Sam?' he asked. 'Is it just Mum? Or is it something else? Maybe school? Can you tell me?'

'You really want to know?'

'I really want to know.'

'But you won't be able to help.'

'I still want to know.'

'OK,' Sam said. 'Actually, I'm in love.'

'Sorry?'

'I know I should be thinking about Mum all the time, and I am. But I'm in love, too, and I was before she died. There's nothing I can do about it …'

'Aren't you a bit young to be in love?'

'No.'

'Right,' said Daniel. 'Well, that's not as bad as I thought.'

'Why?'

'Because I thought it was something worse.'

'Worse than the terrible pain of being in love?'

'Er – no. You're right – terrible pain.'

◆

At the same time, it was the end of the working day at Fairtrade. Sarah was putting her make-up on when Karl came towards her from the other end of the office, passing her desk on his way out.

'Goodnight, Sarah,' he said.

'Goodnight, Karl.'

Karl left. Sarah threw her hands in the air at the thought of her lost opportunity. Then her phone rang.

'Yes,' she said into the phone, 'I'm free. Tell me …'

◆

Jamie had left London, and Katya, for his farmhouse in France. He had just arrived, and his suitcase was still in the middle of the living room. Jamie sat down at a small table and looked sadly at the old-fashioned typewriter in front of him. 'Alone again,' he thought.

◆

Later that same night, the Prime Minister showed one of his ministers out of his office. Natalie was waiting outside.

'Natalie?'

'Sir.'

She came in with a pile of files, put them down and started to leave again.

The Prime Minister spoke. 'Er … I'm starting to feel uncomfortable. We work so closely together all the time, and I know so little about you. It seems wrong.'

'There's not much to know,' Natalie told him.

'Where do you live, for example?'

'Wandsworth. The bad part.'

'My sister lives in Wandsworth. Which, exactly, is the bad part?'

'Right at the end of the High Street,' Natalie told him. 'Harris Street – near the Queen's Head pub.'

'Right, yes, that *is* the bad part. And you live with your husband? Boyfriend? Three lovely children …?'

'No, I've just left my boyfriend, actually, so I'm back with my mum and dad.'

'Oh, I'm sorry,' said the Prime Minister.

'No, that's fine,' said Natalie. 'I'm glad he's gone.' She paused. 'He said I was getting fat.'

'What?'

'He said no one is going to want a girl with legs as big as mine. He wasn't a nice man, actually, in the end.'

The Prime Minister stared at her. 'Right,' he said. He appeared to go back to work, then looked up again. 'You know, as Prime Minister, I could have him murdered.'

'Thank you, sir – I'll think about it.'

'Do that. Trained army killers are just a phone call away.'

They looked at each other and laughed. Then she left.

The Prime Minister looked up at a picture of Margaret Thatcher on the wall. 'Did you have this sort of problem?' he asked it. 'You did, didn't you?'

Chapter 4   The Real World

Back at home, Sam sat on the sofa while Daniel walked round him, thinking hard.

'We can solve this,' he said to his stepson. 'Remember that I was a child too. She's at your school – right?'

'Yes.'

'And how does she feel about you?'

'She doesn't even know my name. And if she did, she'd hate me. Everyone at school thinks she's a goddess.'

'Right,' said Daniel. 'So you've got no chance, have you?'

Sam shook his head sadly.

◆

Billy, the ageing rock star, was being interviewed on a Saturday morning children's TV show by the well-known presenters Ant and Dec.

'So, Billy,' Dec said, 'there are three weeks until Christmas and it looks like the problem's going to be Blue.'

'Yes,' Billy agreed. 'I saw them on the show last week. They weren't very nice about my record.'

'Ah, bad boys!' said Dec. 'Billy, I understand you've got prizes for our competition winners.'

'Yes, I have,' said Billy. 'Big pens with the winners' names on them.'

'Oh, great!' said Ant.

'They're wonderful,' Billy said. 'So if you've got a picture, like this one here of Blue – one of the prizes – you can write on it. Like this.'

Billy wrote a few insulting words about the pop group across the picture. Parents all around the country, shocked by the language, picked up the phone to complain.

'There are lots of children watching, Billy,' Dec said quickly.

'Oh, yes.' Billy nodded. 'Hello, children! Here's an important message from your Uncle Billy. Don't do any schoolwork. Become a pop star, earn lots of money, and drink until you fall over.'

'And now it's time for the advertisements,' Ant told the watching children quickly. 'We'll see you soon. Bye!'

In the next room, Joe hit his head against the wall.

◆

Peter's best man Mark ran an art gallery. Inside the gallery he was on the phone, while three schoolgirls were laughing at a photograph, on the wall, of four large naked bottoms.

Mark covered the phone with his hand and spoke to the girls. 'Actually,' he said. 'They're not funny – they're art.' He spoke into the phone again. 'OK – let's say Thursday, at my place.'

'Great,' said Peter. 'But I've got Juliet here. Can I pass the phone to her? She wants your help.'

'Oh, no,' Mark thought to himself. 'OK – fine,' he said into the phone.

'Thanks. And be nice,' Peter said.

'I'm always nice.'

'You know what I mean, Mark. Be friendly.'

'I'm always …'

'Mark?'

'Hi, Juliet,' Mark said. He paused. 'How was the honeymoon?'

'It was great.'

There was another pause before Mark spoke again. 'So what can I do for you?'

'I need help,' Juliet told him. 'I've played the wedding video and it's all blue and it's got lines across it.'

'I'm sorry.'

'And I remember that you were filming a lot on the day – and I just wondered if I could look at your stuff.'

'Oh, no. I didn't really …'

'Please,' Juliet said. 'I just want one picture of me in a wedding dress that isn't bright blue.'

'OK. I'll have a look,' said Mark. 'But I think I recorded something else over it, so don't get too hopeful. Er … I must go.'

Juliet was left holding the phone.

◆

At Fairtrade, Sarah was sitting at her desk. On the desk, in front of her, was a picture of a good-looking young man.

'Has there been any progress in your love life?' Harry asked.

'No,' Sarah told her boss. 'I've done nothing about it and never will, because he's too good for me.'

'How true,' Harry agreed.

Sarah hit him lightly, and he hit her back. Her phone rang.

'And now, of course, you have a phone call,' said Harry. He turned to Mia. 'How are the arrangements for the Christmas party going?' he asked.

'Good,' Mia replied. 'I think I've found a place. A friend of mine, Mark, works there.'

'What's it like?'

'Good,' said Mia. 'It's an art gallery – full of dark corners for behaving badly in.' She looked at him meaningfully.

'Right,' said Harry. 'Good. Well, I suppose I should see it.'

'You should.'

◆

Jamie was typing when he heard a knock at the front door of his French farmhouse. He opened the door to a middle-aged French woman.

'Good morning, Mr Bennett,' she said, with a strong French accent.

'Hello, Eléonore,' said Jamie.

'Welcome back. And this year, do you have a lady guest?'

'Ah, no. No change there. It's just me.'

'Am I sad about that, or not sad?'

'I think you're not surprised,' Jamie said.

'And you are staying until Christmas?'

'Yes.'

'Good,' said Eléonore. 'And I have found you a perfect lady to clean the house. This is Aurelia.'

Behind Eléonore, another woman stood nervously waiting. She was a pleasant-looking woman in her late twenties.

Jamie stepped forward to greet her. 'Hello, Aurelia,' he said, in careful French.

Aurelia said hello, very quietly, also in French.

Jamie said, very slowly, that he was very happy to have Aurelia there. Confused, Aurelia looked at Eléonore.

'Unfortunately,' Eléonore told Jamie, 'like you, she cannot speak French. She is Portuguese.'

'Ah,' said Jamie, and thought for a minute. Then he wished Aurelia good day in Italian and told her in bad Spanish that Eusebio was a very good footballer.

'She is ten years too young to remember a footballer called Eusebio,' explained Eléonore. 'And "muy bueno" is Spanish.'

'Right,' said Jamie. 'Sure. Well, it's nice to meet you!'

'And perhaps you can drive her home when she finishes her work?' asked Eléonore.

'Of course,' Jamie said. 'Con grande plesoro.'

'What language is that?' asked Eléonore. 'Turkish?'

Later in the day, Jamie drove Aurelia home along an empty road. There was silence in the car and Jamie looked out in embarrassment at the lovely valley they were driving through.

'Beautiful. Beautiful,' he said, in Italian. Aurelia looked confused. 'Mountains,' explained Jamie, in Italian. 'Trees,' he added. Aurelia looked even more confused. 'No, right,' said Jamie to himself. 'Stop talking now.' He continued driving.

Chapter 5   Special Relationships

Outside 10 Downing Street, there were large crowds for the visit of the American President. The car stopped and its doors opened in bright sunshine. The President got out.

The Prime Minister stepped outside and shook hands with him. He seemed quieter and less confident than the American.

'Mr President, welcome,' he said. 'I'm sorry your wife couldn't come.'

'She is too,' smiled the President, 'although it would be rather lonely for her.'

'Because I'm not married?' said the Prime Minister. 'Yes, it's sad, isn't it? I've never been able to get a ring on a girl's finger. I'm not sure politics and women go together.'

'Really? That's not my experience.'

'Well,' the Prime Minister said as they walked into the building, '*you're* very handsome and I look more and more like my Aunt Mildred every day. That's the difference between us.' They walked up the stairs. 'I'm very jealous of your plane,' the Prime Minister added.

The President laughed. 'Thank you. We love it too.'

They passed Natalie.

'Ah, Natalie. Hi,' the Prime Minister said.

'Good morning,' the President said. 'How's your day?'

Natalie smiled and continued down the stairs.

'That is a good-looking girl,' the President said.

'Yes, she's very good … at her job,' said the Prime Minister.

American and British ministers and advisers joined the President and the Prime Minister for a meeting. After some hours, the advisers were still talking and there was no agreement.

'No, no, no,' an American said. 'We cannot and will not discuss that with you.'

'Right,' said Carter, one of the ministers present. 'But we thought you wanted our opinions. This is unexpected.'

'It shouldn't be,' said the President. 'The last American government said the same thing. There are no new ideas here.'

'But if I may say so, sir, we hoped that your government's plans would be better,' Carter told him.

The Prime Minister nodded his agreement. As he had said, though, he didn't want to get into a fight and then lose it.

'Thank you, Alex,' he said to Carter. 'We're not making any progress on this. Let's discuss something else, shall we?'

Later, the President and the Prime Minister sat alone in the Prime Minister's office.

'Well, that was an interesting day,' the Prime Minister said.

'I'm sorry we had to say no to you,' said the President. 'We could say "maybe" now, but then we'd have to say no later. I have plans – and they will succeed.'

'We certainly got that message!' The Prime Minister stood up. 'There's one final thing that I think we should talk about, if you could just give me a second. It's something I feel strongly about.'

'I'll give you anything you ask for,' the President told him, 'unless it's something that I don't want to give.'

The Prime Minister went outside, passing Natalie, who was carrying drinks. He smiled at her shyly.

'Hi,' he said. 'You sad man,' he thought to himself.

Then he went into another office, took some files and walked back.

When he opened the door, he found the President and Natalie standing very close together. The President's hand was around her waist. Natalie went red and moved quickly away, but the President calmly took his glass. For the Prime Minister, for a second, the world seemed to stop.

'Thanks for the drink,' the President said to Natalie.

'I'll go now,' she said, and she walked past the Prime Minister without looking at him.

'Natalie,' the President called out, 'I hope to see much more of you as our two great countries work for a better future.'

'Thank you, sir,' said Natalie.

The Prime Minister looked at the President. He suddenly felt more confident.

The next day, the two leaders took questions from journalists before the President's departure.

'Mr President, has it been a good visit?' a journalist asked.

'Yes, excellent – we got what we came for. Our special relationship is still very special.' The President smiled.

'Prime Minister?' the journalist asked.

There was silence for a moment, and then the Prime Minister

spoke. He looked very serious. 'I love that word "relationship",' he said. 'It can mean anything, can't it? I'm afraid this has become a *bad* relationship. The President takes everything he wants – and doesn't allow the things that matter to Britain. We are a small country, but we're a great one too. A country of Shakespeare, Churchill, the Beatles, Sean Connery, Harry Potter, David Beckham's right foot – and David Beckham's left foot. If a friend bullies us, he stops being our friend. We must be strong, to stop the bullying.' He paused as he saw Natalie in the crowd, at the back of room. 'And from this moment I will be stronger, and the President should be ready for that.'

The journalists were taking photographs and writing fast, excited at having a real story. The other ministers were all smiling.

'Mr President? Mr President? What do you think, sir?' the journalists shouted.

The Prime Minister looked across at him. The President looked back angrily, but with new respect. Then the Prime Minister's eyes turned to Natalie, who looked down at the floor.

The President left, and the ministers were still congratulating the Prime Minister in his office when the telephone rang.

'It's your sister,' the Prime Minister's secretary told him.

He took the phone. 'Yes, I'm very busy and important,' he said. 'How can I help you?'

'Have you gone completely mad?' Karen said.

'You can't be sensible all the time,' the Prime Minister replied.

'You can if you're Prime Minister.'

'Oh, dear. The Minister for Sport is on the other line.'

'No, he isn't.'

'I'll call you back.'

'No, you won't.'

Karen put the phone down and then turned to her husband. 'I'm the Prime Minister's sister,' she said to Harry, 'and so my life looks slightly boring. What did my brother do today? He stood up and fought for his country. And what did I do? I made a paper head for a lobster.'

'What are we listening to?' Harry asked.

'Joni Mitchell.'

'I can't believe you *still* listen to Joni Mitchell.'

'I love her, and true love lasts a lifetime. Joni Mitchell taught your cold wife how to feel.'

'Did she?' said Harry. 'Oh well, that's good. I must write to her some time and thank her.'

◆

A few hours later, in 10 Downing Street, the Prime Minister switched on the radio beside his bed. '… It makes you feel proud to be British,' a voice said. 'So here's a song for our Prime Minister. I think he'll enjoy this.' 'Jump', by the Pointer Sisters, played loudly in the Prime Minister's bedroom. At first the Prime Minister just stood there. Then his arms and feet started to move and he began to dance. He danced out of the door and down the stairs. It had been a good day.

He was still dancing when he noticed his secretary. He stopped. 'Er …' he said, trying to hide his embarrassment. 'Can we move the meeting with the Foreign Secretary to four o'clock tomorrow?'

'Certainly, sir.'

'Good. Thanks very much.'

◆

The next day, Jamie was eating breakfast in his farmhouse in France when Aurelia came in and took his empty coffee cup from a pile of papers. He offered her some cake.

'Would you like some … er …?'

She smiled. Then she spoke, in Portuguese. 'Thank you very much,' she said, refusing the cake, 'but no. If you saw my sister, you'd understand why.'

'That's all right,' Jamie said, in English. 'I'll have it.'

'Just don't eat it all yourself,' Aurelia told him, still in Portuguese. 'You're getting plumper every day.'

'I'm lucky,' said Jamie, who hadn't understood a word she said. 'I can eat as much as I want and I never get fat.'

She looked at him and smiled. His phone rang and, laughing, they both looked for it. In the end they found it between the pages of the book he was writing.

After breakfast, Jamie decided to work in the garden. He took his typewriter outside. Every time he finished a page, he put it under his coffee cup.

Aurelia came out, took away the dirty cup and put down a fresh one.

'Thank you,' Jamie said. But as he spoke, the wind caught his papers. They blew up into the air and then towards the lake at the end of the large garden.

'Oh, no!' screamed Aurelia, in Portuguese. 'Oh, no! I'm so sorry!'

'It's half the book!' Jamie said, worried.

Aurelia caught some of the pages, then ran after the others. She stopped by the edge of the lake.

'Just leave them, please,' Jamie called. 'They're not important.' He stood up and followed her.

Aurelia took off her dress. Jamie thought how lovely she looked in her underwear.

'Stop!' he called to her. 'Please, just leave them.'

Aurelia, of course, didn't understand him, and she dived into the lake.

Jamie ran towards her. 'She'll think I'm not a real man,' he thought, 'if I don't go in too.'

'It's cold!' Aurelia cried.

Jamie stopped for a minute, then took off his trousers and shirt and jumped in. 'It's freezing!' he shouted.

He and Aurelia swam around after the papers.

'This stuff had better be good,' said Aurelia, in Portuguese.

'It isn't Shakespeare,' Jamie told her, in English.

'I don't want to die saving rubbish that my old grandmother could write,' Aurelia said.

'Just stop!' Jamie shouted. 'Stop!'

'What kind of fool doesn't make copies?'

'I really must make copies of my work,' Jamie said. 'I hope there are no fish in here. I hate fish.'

'Try not to step on the fish!'

'Oh! What was that?' Jamie cried, as he stepped on a fish.

A short time later, Jamie entered the living room of the farmhouse with a cup of coffee. Aurelia was in a chair near his table with his jacket over her shoulders.

'Thank you,' Jamie said. 'Thank you very much. I know! I'll name one of the characters after you.'

'Maybe you can put me in your story,' Aurelia said, in Portuguese. 'Or give me 50% of the money you make from it.'

'Or,' Jamie said, thoughtfully, 'I could give you 5% of the money I make from it.'

'What kind of book is it?' She pointed at the wet pages. She pretended to laugh, then cry, and then pointed to her heart.

'Ah,' said Jamie. He made a knife with his fingers.

'Ah, murder,' said Aurelia.

'Yes,' said Jamie. 'Crime. Murder.'

'Frightening?' asked Aurelia. She acted frightened, to show him.

'Sometimes frightening and sometimes not,' he said. 'But the writing is frighteningly bad.'

There was silence for a moment. Neither of them knew what to say next.

'I must get back to work,' said Aurelia. She acted cleaning. 'And then maybe later you will take me home?' She acted driving.

He nodded. They looked at each other.

'It's my favourite time of day, driving you,' Jamie told her.

'It's the saddest part of my day, leaving you,' Aurelia said.

They both looked away.

Chapter 6   Aching Hearts

Mark was at home, watching children's television on a Saturday morning, when he heard the doorbell. He turned off the TV, opened the door and found Juliet there with a large piece of cake in her hand. She had clearly come straight from a bakery.

'Cake?' she offered.

'No, thanks,' he said.

'Good. I find it difficult to share cake.'

'Oh, right.'

'Can I come in?'

'Er … yes. I'm a bit busy, but …'

They went inside.

'I was just passing,' said Juliet, 'and I thought we could check your video. I thought I could exchange it for some cake or …' She pulled sweets from her pocket, '… for some sweets.'

'Actually, I was serious. I don't know where it is. I'll look around tonight and then …'

'Mark, can I say something?'

'Yes.'

'I know you're Peter's best friend,' Juliet began. 'And I know you don't like me very much.' He opened his mouth, but she continued. 'Don't argue. We've never become friends. *But* I hope that can change. I'm nice — I really am. Well, I buy a lot of cake, but it would be good if we could be friends.'

'Yes. Sure. Sure,' Mark said, coldly.

'Great,' said Juliet, feeling hurt.

'But that doesn't mean we'll be able to find the video. I had a good look when you first called and I couldn't see it, so I'll have to …'

'There's a video here that says "Peter and Juliet's Wedding" on it. Could that possibly be it?'

'Ah, yes,' said Mark. 'Well … yes.'

She moved towards the TV and put the video in the machine.

'I've probably recorded something on top of it,' Mark told her. 'All my videos have *West Wing* on them now.'

She sat down as the video started to play. He stayed on his feet. There Juliet was, walking down the centre of the church.

'Oh great! That's lovely!' Juliet cried. 'This is just what I was hoping for. I look quite pretty.' Mark stood silently as, again and again, Juliet's face appeared on the screen. 'You've stayed rather close to me, haven't you?' she said slowly.

They watched in silence as it became clear that there was only one person in this wedding video. Finally, there was Juliet leaving for her honeymoon, waving goodbye.

'The whole video,' she said. 'All me.'

'Yes,' Mark said. 'Yes.'

'But you never talk to me,' Juliet said. 'You always talk to Peter. You don't like me.'

Mark didn't know what to say. 'I hope it's useful,' he said, finally. 'Don't show it to too many people. It needs cutting. Now, I've got to meet someone for … lunch. An early lunch. Sorry.' He walked towards the door and then turned back. 'I don't want to get hurt,' he said. 'Do you understand that?'

He left without waiting for an answer.

Outside the house he walked away, then turned back, then walked away again.

♦

There was a knock on the door of the Prime Minister's office and Annie came in.

'Annie, my love, my sweet, my dream, I need you to do something for me.'

'Of course. What would our country's hero like?' Annie said.

'Don't ask me why, but ... you know Natalie, who works here?'

'The plump one?'

'Do you think she's plump?'

'I think her bottom's quite big, yes, sir. And she has very fat legs.'

'Right. Well, I'm sure she's a lovely girl, but ... could you find her work somewhere else?'

'Of course.'

The Prime Minister looked out of the window for a minute. Then he sat down at his desk and started to write.

He had worked for hours when there was another knock at the door. He jumped.

'Yes – come in.'

The door opened and a girl came in with tea. It wasn't Natalie.

'Prime Minister,' the woman said.

'Thank you.'

He looked at her and realized sadly what he had done.

◆

Late the same night, Daniel was in his office at home, staring at a picture of his dead wife. As the door opened and his stepson came in, he tried to look more cheerful.

'Hi, Sam. Can't sleep?'

'I got some terrible news today,' Sam told him.

'What is it?'

'Joanna's going back to America.'

'Your girl is American?'

'Yes,' said Sam. 'She's American and she's not my girl, and she's going back to America and that's the end of my life.'

'That *is* bad news,' Daniel agreed. 'We need Kate and we need Leo.'

They went into the living room and put a video on. *Titanic*, starring Leonardo DiCaprio and Kate Winslet, came on in the middle of the film.

'Do you trust me?' Leo's character was asking, up at the front of the ship.

'I trust you,' Kate answered.

They stood there with their arms out, like birds flying.

Daniel and Sam put their arms out too. Daniel stood behind Sam.

'Do you trust me?' he asked his stepson.

'I trust you,' Sam said.

'Fool!' Daniel pushed him down onto the sofa and they lay back, laughing.

'You know, Sam,' Daniel told him, 'I'm sure she's a great girl. But most people believe there isn't just one person for each of us.'

'There was for Kate and Leo. There was for you. There is for me. She's the one,' Sam replied.

'Right … And her name's Joanna?'

'Yes. Like Mum.'

Daniel thought about this.

◆

The next day, Jamie left his French farmhouse to return to England for Christmas. Aurelia helped him fill every corner of the car with wine, cheese and other presents for his family.

'Apologia,' Jamie said, in no known language. 'Grande familio. Grande tradizione di Christmas presents stupidos.'

He drove Aurelia to the edge of town for the last time before the holiday. Then he got out of the car and put out his hand. She took it.

'Well, goodbye,' he said.

'Thank you,' said Aurelia, in Portuguese. 'I will miss you, and your very slow writing, and your very bad driving.'

He smiled at her without understanding. She gave him a gentle kiss on the mouth, and then walked away.

Jamie thought for a moment and then got back into the car. He started the car and moved out into the road without looking. A car drove into the back of his.

◆

Through the window of a record shop, Sam watched a video of Billy Mack's Christmas song. Behind Billy, seven girls dressed in red and white were dancing enthusiastically.

Suddenly, Sam turned and ran home.

'Daniel! I've got a plan!' he shouted, as he ran into his stepfather's office.

'Thank God,' Daniel said. 'Tell me.'

'Girls love musicians, don't they? Even the really strange men get girlfriends.'

'That's right. Ringo Starr married a girl from a James Bond film.'

'Right. There's a big concert soon at school, and Joanna's in it. If I'm in a rock group and play really wonderfully, she might actually fall in love with me. What do you think?'

'I think it's a great idea. There's just one small problem ...'

'That I don't play a musical instrument?'

'Yes.'

'That's *so* unimportant.'

Later that evening, as he was walking past Sam's room to bed, Daniel heard the sound of drumming. Sam was teaching himself to play.

◆

It was a cold evening, but Mark's art gallery was warm, music was playing, and everybody was having a good time at Fairtrade's Christmas party.

Karl was getting a drink. Sarah stood nervously alone beside a large photo of a naked woman.

'I'll go round and talk to everybody, shall I?' Karen asked her husband.

'You're wonderful,' said Harry.

Suddenly Mia was there next to him, looking wonderful in a tight red dress. 'Is there any chance of a dance with the boss?'

'Yes, sure ... if your boyfriend doesn't mind.'

'I haven't got a boyfriend,' Mia said.

Karen talked sweetly to a very dull couple, but her eyes were on her husband and Mia.

'You're looking very ... pretty tonight,' Harry told Mia.

There was silence for a second. 'It's for you,' Mia said.

'Sorry?'

'It's all for you ... sir.'

Karen moved on to talk to Sarah and they both watched Harry and Mia.

'I suppose it's his job to dance with everyone, isn't it?' Sarah said, softly.

'Yes – but some more than others,' Karen replied.

Karl appeared beside them. 'Just one dance?' he asked.

'Who – me?' asked Sarah.

'Unless you ...'

'No, no,' Sarah said. 'Good ... yes ... thanks.'

As they started to dance, a slow, romantic song began to play.

◆

That evening, Billy was being interviewed by Michael Parkinson, a very famous TV presenter.

'Well, this must be a very exciting moment for you,' Parkinson said. 'You are fighting for the Christmas Number One. How's it going?'

'Very badly. Blue are selling five times more CDs than I am. But

I'm hoping that sales will improve. And if I reach Number One in the charts, I promise to sing the song naked on TV.'

'Do you mean that?' Parkinson asked.

'Of course I mean it. Look.'

Billy stood up, faced the presenter and opened his trousers.

'That will never reach Number One,' Parkinson laughed.

♦

Much later, Karl said good night to Sarah in the hall of the building where her flat was.

'Well, I'd better go,' he said.

'OK.'

'Good night.'

'Good night,' Sarah replied.

Karl kissed her – on the cheek and then on the lips. 'I don't actually have to go,' he said.

'Right,' said Sarah. 'Good. That's good.' She tried not to show her pleasure. 'Would you excuse me one second?' She went outside, screamed silently, and jumped up and down with excitement. Then she went back inside. 'Right,' she said. 'Why don't you come upstairs in about ten seconds?'

She was tidying the flat when Karl entered. He took off his coat and waited. Then they ran towards each other and kissed. Clothes fell to the floor.

'You're beautiful,' he told her.

As they kissed again, the phone rang.

Sarah paused. 'I'd better answer it,' she said sadly. She pushed him away and covered herself. 'Hello, darling ... No, I'm not busy.' Karl looked at her, surprised and a little hurt. 'Right ... Right ... Yes,' Sarah continued. 'I'm not sure it's going to be possible to phone the Queen tonight but ... Yes, yes ... I'm sure she'll be interested.' She moved further away from Karl. 'OK,' she said. 'I'll talk to you later. Bye bye.' She put the phone down. 'I'm sorry about that.'

'No, it's fine,' Karl said.

'It was my brother. He's not well. He calls a lot.'

'I'm sorry.'

'No, it's fine,' said Sarah. 'I mean, it's not really fine – but we've got no parents now and it's my job to … help him if I can. Well, not "job". I'm glad to do it.'

'That's OK,' Karl said. 'Life is full of interruptions and difficulties. So …' He kissed her.

The phone rang again. They both looked at it.

'Will it make him better?' Karl asked.

'No.'

'Then maybe … don't answer?'

There was silence for a minute as Sarah looked at Karl. Then she picked up the phone.

'Hey, how are you doing? Right … Right.' Karl sat quietly beside her. 'Little darling,' said Sarah, 'please don't. We're going to find the answer between us and it won't hurt any more …' Karl put his head in his hands, waiting. 'No,' said Sarah, 'I'm not busy. If you want me to come now, of course I will. … OK …' She looked at Karl.

◆

In the early morning, after the Fairtrade Christmas party had ended, Karen and Harry were in their bedroom.

'That was a good night,' said Karen, 'although I felt fat.'

'Oh, don't be silly,' Harry said.

'It's true.' She took off her dress, shyly. 'I can only wear clothes now that used to belong to Pavarotti.'

Harry watched her. 'I think Pavarotti dresses very well.'

'Mia's very pretty.'

'Is she?'

'You know she is, darling,' said Karen. 'Be careful.'

◆

Sarah, at that moment, was visiting her brother in a special hospital. The cold, lonely room had very little furniture in it and a large male nurse stood by the door.

Michael was paler and thinner and had dirtier hair than in the photograph on Sarah's desk.

'Have you been watching TV?' Sarah asked him.

'No … Yes. Every night.'

'Oh, good.'

'Every day. The nurses are trying to kill me.'

'Nobody's trying to kill you, darling.'

Michael was silent. Then he suddenly lifted his hand to hit her. The nurse stepped towards her to protect her, but Sarah took Michael's hand.

'Don't do that, my darling,' she said, very gently.

◆

On the day after the party, everyone at Fairtrade was quieter than usual. Harry was talking to Mia.

'Right,' he said. 'I'll be back at three. I'm going Christmas shopping – never an easy or a pleasant job.'

'Are you going to get me something?'

'Er … I don't know. I hadn't thought.' They stared at each other. 'Where's Sarah?' he asked.

'She couldn't come in today,' said Mia. 'A family problem.'

'You mean, she drank too much last night? See you later.'

'Yes. I'll be waiting for you. Any time.'

Harry left the office, very confused about his feelings. He walked down a busy street, decorated with Christmas trees and Christmas lights everywhere. He thought for a second and then took out his phone and called.

'Are *you* going to give *me* something?' he asked.

'I thought you understood last night,' said Mia. 'You can have everything. All of me.'

Harry was shocked. 'So … er … this Christmas present. What do you need? Something for the office? Pens perhaps? A ruler?'

'No,' said Mia. 'I don't want something I need. I want something I want. Something pretty.'

'Right … right.' Harry turned his phone off. Then he saw his wife in the crowd and waved.

'Sorry I'm late,' said Karen. 'I had to take Bernie to school. There's a rehearsal for the Christmas play.' They went into one of London's biggest shops. 'Look after yourself for ten minutes while I get some boring stuff for our mothers,' Karen said, and disappeared into the crowd.

Harry looked around and saw some jewellery. He stared at it for a minute or two, thinking.

'Are you looking for something special?' the assistant asked him.

'Yes … er … How much is that necklace?' he asked, finally, pointing at one with a gold heart hanging from it.

'It's £270,' said the assistant.

Harry thought about spending all that money on a woman who was not his wife. 'All right. I'll have it,' he said, quickly.

'I'll put it in some nice Christmas paper,' the assistant said.

'Yes, all right.'

The assistant took the necklace and put it carefully in a box.

'Listen. Could we be quite quick?' Harry said.

'Certainly, sir. I won't be long.' The assistant took out some paper and put it around the box. 'There,' he said.

'That's great.'

'I haven't quite finished,' the assistant told him. He took out a bag.

'I don't really need a bag,' Harry said nervously. 'I can put it in my pocket.'

'This isn't an ordinary bag,' the assistant told him. 'Look.' He took out some little dried roses and put them carefully into the bag with the necklace. Then he opened another drawer.

'Actually, I really can't wait,' Harry said.

'You won't be sorry,' the assistant said, as he put more dried flowers into the bag.

'I might,' Harry told him, looking around him.

'Just a few more seconds,' the assistant said. He tied the top of the bag and then opened his drawer again.

'Have you almost finished?' Harry asked. 'What now? Are you going to cover it with chocolate?'

'No, sir. I'm going to put it in this Christmas box.'

'I don't want a Christmas box!'

'But it's a gift, isn't it?'

'Yes, but … Can I just pay?'

'Well, I just need …'

'No! No!'

'But sir …'

'Leave it – leave it, just leave it.'

'Ah, looking at the jewellery, are you?' Karen said, appearing beside him.

Harry moved quickly away. 'No, I hate jewellery.'

'Don't worry,' Karen said. 'I don't expect much after thirteen years, Mr But-You-Always-Love-Chocolate-At-Christmas.'

◆

In another part of London, in a large, brightly lit room, students from around the world were learning English. They sat at their desks listening to cassettes through earphones.

'Sherlock Holmes is not a real detective,' one student repeated carefully.

'Is this the way to the train station?' a Russian student translated into her own language.

'I would like a kilo of oranges,' another one said, in English.

'I would like a one-day travel card,' said a fourth student seriously.

At one of the desks, Jamie was learning Portuguese. 'I've got a terrible stomach ache,' he said slowly, in Portuguese. 'I think it was the fish.'

When he left the building and entered the underground station, he was still talking to himself in Portuguese.

'This is a very big fish!' he said loudly. 'It tastes wonderful!'

◆

'Has she noticed you yet?' Daniel asked Sam.

'No, not yet. But romantic films are like that, aren't they? People only come together at the end.'

'Of course,' Daniel agreed.

'I feel bad that I never ask you how your love life's going,' Sam said seriously.

'Ha! I've finished with all that,' Daniel said. 'Unless, of course, Claudia Schiffer calls.'

Chapter 7   The Night Before Christmas

It was the evening before Christmas, and Karen was allowing each member of the family to open one of their presents.

'Why don't you take one for yourself?' Harry asked her.

'Maybe I will,' said Karen. 'I think I want this one.' She smiled as she picked up a small, flat box, a present from Harry.

'I have, of course, bought the traditional chocolates too,' Harry told her. 'But this is my other … slightly special, personal gift.'

'Thank you,' Karen said. She opened it, full of excitement. Then the excitement left her. 'That's a surprise. It's a CD – Joni Mitchell.'

'To continue your emotional improvement,' her husband said.

'That's great.'

'My wonderful wife.'

'Ha! Yes. Actually, I'll have to leave the room for a moment. All that ice-cream. Darling, could you make sure the children are ready to go? I'll be back in a minute.'

She left the room slowly, trying hard to keep the smile on her face.

◆

At the same time, a radio DJ was talking to the nation. 'It's raining all over the UK,' he said. 'And the big question is – who is Number One in the charts tonight? Is it Blue, or the unexpected success from Billy Mack? Well, you probably guessed, although you may not believe it. It's … Billy Mack!'

At Billy's record company, where everyone was still in the office, the noise from the celebrations was deafening.

'You are the best!' Joe shouted.

The phone rang and the room went quiet as Billy answered, standing on a table in the middle of the room.

'Hello,' he said.

'Hello, Billy,' the DJ said. 'We're live across the nation and you're Number One. How will you celebrate?'

'I don't know. Either I'll get drunk with my fat manager or, when I put the phone down, I'll be invited to a lot of wonderful parties by rich and famous people.'

'Let's hope it's the parties,' said the DJ. 'And here it is – Number One, from Billy Mack … It's "Christmas Is All Around".'

'Oh no!' said Billy. 'Not that rubbish again!' He put the phone down.

Gina, a young manager at the record company, stepped forward, holding her phone. 'Billy – it's for you, darling.'

Billy took the phone. 'Hello. Elton? Of course. Of course. Of course. Send an embarrassingly big car and I'll be there.' He gave the phone back to Gina. 'It's going to be a very good Christmas,' he said.

Joe smiled at him, looking rather lost among all Billy's new friends.

◆

Jamie stood at his parents' front door with his hands full of Christmas presents and rang the door bell. The door opened.

'Look, everyone, it's Jamie!' his sister called back into the house.

His father, mother, sisters, brothers and their children all came to greet him excitedly.

'Lovely to see you all,' said Jamie, putting down the presents and kissing everybody. 'But I've got to go now.'

'But Jamie, darling …' said his mother, shocked.

'Sorry,' Jamie said. 'There are some things that a man just has to do.'

He gave his sister the bags of presents and left. Then he took a taxi to Gatwick Airport.

◆

Karl and Sarah were the only two people left in the Fairtrade office. Karl stood up to leave.

'Good night, Sarah,' he said.

'Good night, Karl.'

'I …' Karl stopped. 'Happy Christmas.'

Sarah smiled at him. 'Happy Christmas.'

As Karl left, Sarah reached for her phone and rang a number.

'Hi, darling,' she said, trying to sound cheerful. 'How are you? Is it party-time down there?'

Half an hour later she was at the hospital, opening presents with her brother.

'I love you, Michael,' Sarah said.

'I know,' said Michael. He paused. 'I love you too.'

◆

Karen stood in her bedroom, listening to her new CD. As Joni Mitchell sang about the pain of love, tears ran down her face.

Then she forced herself to stop crying, put a smile on her face, and went back to join her family.

◆

Peter and Juliet were watching TV when their doorbell rang. Juliet went downstairs and opened the door to Mark.

'Oh! Hi,' she said.

'Who is it?' Peter called from the living room.

Mark put his fingers to his lips and held up a big white card with a message on it: 'Say it's carol singers.'

'It's carol singers,' Juliet called.

'Well, give them a pound and tell them to go away,' Peter shouted.

Mark pushed the button on a CD player. At the sound of children singing Christmas carols, Juliet laughed.

Then Mark held up other cards: 'If I'm lucky next year,' the first one said. He pulled out the second. 'I'll be with one of these girls.' The third card showed pictures of the four most beautiful women in the world. 'But I just want to say,' the cards continued, 'that to me you are perfect. And my poor heart will love you … until you look like this.' Mark held up a picture of a very old woman. Then he showed a final card that said 'Happy Christmas'.

He picked up the CD player and started to walk away, but Juliet followed him and kissed him gently on the lips.

Mark smiled. 'Enough,' he said. 'Enough now.'

◆

Later in the evening, Joe was drinking alone in his flat, watching Billy's video on TV, when his doorbell rang.

'What are you doing here?' he said, as he opened the door. 'Why aren't you at Elton John's?'

'I was there for a minute or two,' Billy told him. 'And then I had a life-changing experience.'

'Really? Come in,' said Joe. 'And what was this life-changing experience?' he asked, when they were inside.

'It was about Christmas,' said Billy.

'You realized that it was all around?'

'No, I realized that at Christmas you should be with the people you love.'

'Right.'

'And I realized that I am in my fifties and I have actually spent most of my adult life with a fat manager. And, sadly, it is clear to me that you are, in fact, the person I love.'

'Well, this is a surprise.'

'Yes.'

'Ten minutes with Elton John and suddenly you're in love with a man.'

'No, I'm serious. I left Elton's place, and all those beautiful girls, to be with you. At Christmas.'

There was a second's silence. 'Well, Billy …'

'We've had a wonderful life together.'

'Well, thank you! Thanks, man. I feel very proud.'

The two men put their arms round each other.

'That's enough!' Billy said. 'Let's get drunk and watch videos of naked women.'

Chapter 8   The Christmas Concert

In 10 Downing Street, the Prime Minister was alone – very alone. He looked through his Christmas cards.

First, he read a couple of boring ones. He couldn't even read the signature on one of them. The third card gave him a shock. It was from Natalie.

Dear Sir – Dear David,

Happy Christmas and I hope you have a very Happy New Year. I'm very sorry about the thing that happened. It was a very odd moment and I feel like a complete fool. Especially because (if you can't say it at Christmas, when can you?) I'm actually yours, with LOVE, Your Natalie

The Prime Minister paused for a moment, put the card down, read it again and then made up his mind. He picked up a phone and pushed a button. 'Jack,' he said. 'I need a car. Now. Thank you.' Then he left the room, ran to his waiting car and told the driver to go to Harris Street, Wandsworth.

When the Prime Minister's car stopped in Harris Street, the police car behind it stopped too.

The Prime Minister's driver turned to him. 'Here we are. What number, sir?'

'I have no idea, and it's the longest street in the world.'

The Prime Minister got out of the car and rang the doorbell of number 1. An old lady opened the door.

'Hello,' the Prime Minister said. 'Does Natalie live here?'

'No,' said the old lady.

'Right,' said the Prime Minister. 'Fine. Thank you for your help. Goodbye.'

'Aren't you the Prime Minister?' the old lady asked.

'Yes – in fact I am. Happy Christmas. This is just part of the service. I'm hoping to see everyone by the end of the year.'

The Prime Minister rang the next doorbell, as the cars followed slowly. Three small girls answered.

'Hello. Does Natalie live here?' the Prime Minister asked.

'No,' said the oldest girl. 'Are you singing Christmas carols?'

'Er … No. I'm not.'

'Please, sir, please,' the second child said.

'Please,' said the third.

'Er … All right.'

The Prime Minister waved at his bodyguard, who sang with him as the children danced to the music.

'We wish you a Happy Christmas,' they sang loudly. 'We wish you a Happy Christmas, we wish you a Happy Christmas and a Happy New Year!'

The Prime Minister knocked on the next door and Mia opened it, wearing the beautiful necklace with the gold heart that Harry had bought her.

'Hello. Excuse me,' said the Prime Minister. 'Does Natalie live here?'

'No,' Mia said. 'She's next door. You're not who I think you are, are you?'

'Yes, I'm afraid I am. Sorry about all the mistakes. My ministers are complete fools, but we hope to do better next year. Happy Christmas.'

The Prime Minister combed his hair, walked slowly to the door of Natalie's house and rang the bell. The door opened, and members of the family were crowded in the hall, ready to go out. Natalie wasn't with them.

'Hello,' said the Prime Minister. 'Is Natalie there?'

Natalie was just coming down the stairs, but she hadn't noticed him. 'Has anyone seen my coat?' she shouted. Then she saw him. 'Oh, hello,' she said.

'Hello,' said the Prime Minister.

'This is my mum and my dad,' Natalie introduced them. 'And my Uncle Tony and Aunt Glynne ...'

'Pleased to meet you,' said the Prime Minister.

'And this is ... the Prime Minister,' Natalie told them.

'Yes, we can see that, darling,' said Natalie's mother.

'And unfortunately we're very late,' Natalie said.

'It's the schools' Christmas concert, David,' said Natalie's mother. 'And it's the first time all the schools have done it together, even St Basil's, which is very ...'

'Too much detail, Mum,' Natalie told her.

'So, ... er ... how can we help, sir?' Natalie's father asked.

'Well, actually, I need to talk to Natalie ... about something of national importance.'

'Right, yes – of course,' said Natalie's father, looking at his watch. 'Perhaps you could come along later, Fatty – er, Natalie.'

'No – I don't want you to miss the concert,' the Prime Minister said to Natalie.

'It doesn't matter,' said Natalie.

'Keith will be really upset,' her mother said.

'No, really – it doesn't matter,' Natalie repeated.

'It hasn't been easy making him look like a really good lobster. Lobsters are such a difficult colour, aren't they?' her mother said to the Prime Minister.

'Why don't I drive you, Natalie? We can talk about ... this business in the car.'

'OK,' Natalie smiled.

'Lovely,' her parents agreed.

'How far is this place?' the Prime Minister asked, when Natalie and her brother Keith were in the car with his driver and the bodyguard. The rest of the family had crowded into the police car.

'Just round the corner,' Natalie said.

'Right,' said the Prime Minister. 'Well, I just wanted to say thank you for the Christmas card.'

'You're welcome,' said Natalie. 'Listen, I'm so sorry about that day. I came into the room, and he came towards me, and he's the President of the United States and ... nothing happened, I promise. I felt such a fool because I think about you all the time, and I think you're the man I really ...'

'We're here,' Keith said.

'Love,' Natalie whispered.

The Prime Minister didn't hear her. 'Ah,' he said as the car stopped. 'It really was round the corner, wasn't it? Listen, I don't think I'll come in. Everybody should be watching the children, not a hated politician.'

'No, please come. It'll be great.'

'No, I'd better not. But I will be very sorry to drive away from you.'

'Just give me one second …' Natalie said.

She opened the car door and ran out into the car park, past Daniel and Sam, who were just arriving. Sam was carrying drumsticks and Daniel was trying to flatten Sam's hair.

Natalie was back quickly. 'Come on,' she said. 'We can watch from behind the stage.'

'OK,' said the Prime Minister. And then, to his driver, 'Terry, I won't be long.'

As they got out of the car with the bodyguard, he paused. 'This has to be a very *private* visit, OK?' he whispered.

'Don't worry,' Natalie said. 'This was my school. I know the way.' She led him away from the crowd to a side door.

Karen and her family arrived at the school concert soon afterwards. As they hurried towards the big hall, they met the Prime Minister and Natalie, who were going the other way.

'David!' Karen said. She gave her brother a kiss, and he saw immediately that she was upset.

'How are you?' he asked, waving at the children. 'Are you all right?'

'What are you doing here?' Karen asked.

'Well …'

'I always tell your secretary's secretary's secretary that these things are happening – but I didn't think you'd actually come.'

'Well, it's a long story and I didn't want everyone to see, so I'm just going to hide myself somewhere and watch. Good luck, Daisy! Good luck, Bernie!'

'I've never been gladder to see my stupid big brother,' Karen said. 'Thank you for coming!'

'You're welcome,' said the Prime Minister.

'Aren't you going to introduce me?' Karen asked, nodding at Natalie, who was standing with the bodyguard.

'This is Natalie,' the Prime Minister said. 'She's in charge of ... the food at 10 Downing Street.'

'Well, make sure he keeps his hands off you,' Karen warned Natalie. 'Twenty years ago, he really liked girls like you.'

They all laughed.

'I'll be careful,' said Natalie. And then, to the Prime Minister, 'Don't try anything, sir, just because it's Christmas.'

Karen gave her brother a final kiss as she and her family went to their seats.

'See you later.'

'Yes, probably.'

'Thank you, Prime Minister,' she said.

The school concert was a big success. Jesus, Mary, Joseph, the cows, sheep, lobsters and other sea animals performed well in the Christmas play. Even Spiderman appeared on stage, although nobody was sure why.

Natalie and the Prime Minister watched together, through a curtain behind the stage.

Near the end of the concert, one of the teachers went up onto the stage. 'Hiller School would now like to sing for you,' he said. 'Ten-year-old Joanna Anderson will lead the singing.'

A small girl came up onto the stage and started singing, in a beautiful voice. Teachers and other pupils joined in the Mariah Carey song, 'All I Want For Christmas Is You'. Behind them, Sam beat his drums enthusiastically.

As, behind the stage, the Prime Minister and Natalie moved closer to each other, the parents in front of the stage stood up.

Joanna sang the title line for the last time. On the word 'you', she pointed at Sam. Sam gave a smile of pleasure, which disappeared as Joanna turned again to the front.

46

At the end of the song, paper snow poured down onto the stage. Then the back curtain opened to show a painted Christmas scene – and the Prime·Minister and Natalie kissing. Every parent in the school lifted their camera.

'Ah!' the Prime Minister whispered to Natalie. 'This is not *quite* as private as we'd hoped.'

'What do we do now?' Natalie whispered.

'Smile.' They smiled at the excited parents. 'And wave.'

They waved. Then they left the stage.

Chapter 9   Love Actually Is All Around

At the end of the school concert, Karen said goodbye to some other parents while Harry waited for her. Then she turned to her husband.

'Tell me,' she said. 'What would you do, in my situation?'

'What situation is that?'

'Imagine your husband bought a necklace with a gold heart on it at Christmas and gave it to somebody else.'

'Oh, Karen.'

'Would you wait to find out if it's just a necklace – or if it's sex and a necklace – or, worst of all, if it's a necklace and love? Would you stay, knowing that life will always be a bit worse now? Or would you get out?'

'Oh God, I've been such a complete fool.'

'Yes, but you've also made a fool of me – and made my life foolish too.'

Daisy and Bernie ran up to them, pleased with themselves after the success of the concert, and Karen became a mother again.

'Bernie, darling, you were wonderful,' she told her son. And then, to Daisy, 'And my little lobster, you were so … orange. Let's go home.'

Daniel found Sam. 'Sam! Great show. You were wonderful on drums, son.'

'Thanks,' said Sam. 'The plan didn't work, though.'

'So tell her,' said Daniel.

'Tell her what?'

'Tell her you love her.'

'No!' said Sam. 'And they fly home tonight.'

'Even better,' said his stepfather. 'You've got nothing to lose. I never told your Mum enough that I loved her. Not every day, and she was perfect every day. You've seen the films. There's always a chance at the last moment.'

Sam thought for a moment. 'OK – let's do it, Dad. Just give me one second.'

He ran off. A mother and her son walked into Daniel.

'Sorry,' said the mother, who looked exactly like Claudia Schiffer.

'That's OK. My fault,' said Daniel.

'No, really, it wasn't. You're Sam's dad, aren't you?'

'Yes. Well, I'm his stepfather. Daniel.'

'I'm Carol.'

They looked at each other.

'OK, I'm back,' Sam said. 'Let's go.'

'Yes ... er ... I hope we meet again, Karen.'

'Carol. I'll make sure we do.'

'Yes, good.'

As they walked away, Sam said, 'Tell her.'

'Tell her what?'

'You know.' He made a kissing noise.

'Don't be so silly,' Daniel told him.

Outside in the school car park, they looked around them.

'There she is,' Sam said.

'Where?'

'There.'

Joanna was getting into a big car, which then drove away.

'Oh no,' Sam said.

'Don't worry,' said Daniel. 'We can get to the airport before them. I know a way.'

They ran to Daniel's car and drove off fast.

When they finally arrived at Heathrow Airport, Daniel and Sam ran inside and looked up at the board.

'New York – Gate 36 – last call,' it said.

'Oh, no!' Sam cried.

They ran to the entrance to the departure area.

'We're not actually flying,' Daniel explained to the airport official.

'You can't come through here without a boarding pass,' the man told them.

'Not even for the boy to say goodbye to the love of his life?'

'No.'

'I'm sorry, Sam,' Daniel said sadly.

A passenger appeared beside them.

'Boarding pass, sir,' the official said.

The passenger started looking for his pass. 'Just a minute. I know it's here somewhere. Could you hold my coat and bag? Thank you. Now perhaps …'

'Do you want to try?' Daniel whispered to Sam.

'Should I?' Sam whispered back.

The airport official was watching the passenger now, and his hands were full. Sam ran past him unnoticed.

'I'm sorry,' the passenger was explaining. 'Perhaps I left it in the coffee shop.'

Sam ran past the machines where passengers' bags were checked and jumped over another official, who was examining the bottom of a man's trousers. A guard tried to stop him, but failed. Sam ran past the shops.

At Gate 36, Joanna was just preparing to board the plane. There were guards between Sam and her, but their eyes were on a television screen. On it, Billy Mack was singing 'Christmas Is All Around' while taking all his clothes off.

Sam ran past the guards.

The guards turned and ran after him.

'Joanna!' Sam called.

'Sam?' said Joanna.

'I thought you didn't know my name,' Sam said.

'Of course I do.'

The guards had arrived.

'I've got to run,' Sam told her.

The guards led him out of the departure area towards Daniel, who was waiting anxiously.

As Sam waved at Daniel, he felt a hand on his shoulder and turned. Joanna kissed him on the cheek and then ran back to her plane.

Sam went happily to Daniel, who lifted him high into the air.

♦

In a poor part of Marseille, in the south of France, Jamie's taxi stopped in a narrow, dirty street. He got out and knocked on a door. A big man of about sixty opened it.

'Good evening, Mr Barros,' Jamie said, in Portuguese. 'I would like to marry your daughter. I hope that you will give me your permission.'

'You wish to marry my daughter?'

'Yes.'

Mr Barros called back, into the house. 'Come here quickly! There is a man at the door.'

A very large Portuguese girl came through a plastic curtain from the next room.

'He wants to marry you, Sophia,' Mr Barros told his daughter.

'But I've never met him before,' Sophia replied.

'That doesn't matter,' her father said.

'You're going to sell me to a complete stranger?'

'Sell? Who said "sell"? I'll pay him to take you.'

A neighbour, an old lady, appeared on the stairs to listen.

'Ah, excuse me,' said Jamie, still in Portuguese, but making mistakes now. 'I mean your other daughter, Aurelia.'

'Aurelia is not here,' Mr Barros told Jamie. 'She's at work. I'll take you.' He turned to Sophia. 'You! Stay here!'

'No!' said Sophia.

All four of them, including the old lady, started walking down the street. They passed a small restaurant where a family was having dinner.

'Father is going to sell Aurelia to this Englishman,' Sophia informed the family.

The family left their dinner and followed. They didn't want to miss this. More and more people joined them, as the story of Jamie and Aurelia grew and changed.

'They say he is going to kill Aurelia,' one child told another.

About forty people were now walking through the streets of Marseille.

'Great!' the second child said happily.

A fruit-seller at the side of the road stopped selling fruit and joined them. Finally, the whole crowd followed Mr Barros into a small Portuguese restaurant.

Mr Barros spoke to the owner. 'Where is Aurelia?'

'Why should I tell you?'

'This man wants to marry her.'

'He can't do that,' said the owner. 'She's our best waitress.'

At that moment Aurelia appeared, holding plates of food. She saw Jamie and her eyes widened. She put the plates down.

'Good evening, Aurelia,' Jamie said, in Portuguese.

'Good evening, Jamie,' she replied.

There was silence. The whole restaurant was listening now.

'Beautiful Aurelia,' Jamie began in slow, careful Portuguese. 'I have come here to ask you to be my wife. I know I seem mad because I don't really know you, but everything is clear to me. We can live here or you can live with me in England.'

'Choose England,' Sophia advised. 'You might meet Prince William, and then you can marry him instead.'

'Ssssh!' Mr Barros told her crossly.

Aurelia said nothing.

'Of course I don't expect you to say yes,' Jamie continued. 'But it's Christmas and I wanted to ... check.'

'Say yes, you undersized fool,' said Sophia.

'Thank you,' Aurelia said, very slowly, in English. 'That will be nice. "Yes" is my answer. Easy question.'

'What did you say?' Mr Barros asked his daughter.

'Yes, of course,' Aurelia replied in Portuguese.

'You learnt English?' Jamie asked.

'I thought ... maybe ...'

They kissed. Then Sophia pulled Jamie away from her sister and kissed him loudly on the mouth. Their father did the same.

◆

A month later, at Heathrow Airport, a lot of people were leaving the Arrivals Hall.

As Billy came through the gate with a beautiful, tall girl, Joe stepped out of the waiting crowd to meet him.

'Hello, Daisy,' he said.

'This one's Greta,' Billy told him.

'Hello, Greta.'

Jamie arrived next, with Aurelia. He introduced her to Peter and Juliet. 'Oh, and Mark!' he said. 'Hi! I didn't see you.'

Mark was looking at the floor. 'Yes ... I thought I'd come too.'

'Jamie's friends are so good-looking,' Aurelia said, in English. 'He didn't tell me this. I think now maybe I have made the wrong choice – chosen the wrong Englishman.'

'She can't speak English very well. She doesn't know what she's saying,' Jamie said.

They all laughed and walked away.

Harry came out and looked around. Yes, Karen was there, with Daisy and Bernie. The children held a big sign with 'Welcome Home Dad' on it.

Harry looked shyly at Karen. Then he kissed her. 'How are you?' he asked.

'I'm fine, I'm fine,' she said. 'Good to have you back,' she said formally. She turned to the children. 'Come on – home,' she said.

Joanna arrived, with her family.

'There she is!' Sam cried. He ran up to her, then stopped and shook her hand.

'Hi,' Joanna said.

'Hello.'

'Why doesn't he kiss her?' Daniel whispered to Carol, who was standing beside him.

'They've got time,' Carol reminded him.

Suddenly, there were journalists and cameras everywhere. The Prime Minister came through the gate, surrounded by bodyguards.

Natalie ran through the crowd, put her arms round him and held him tightly. Then she jumped up into his arms and put her legs round his waist.

'You're so heavy!' the Prime Minister told Natalie.

'Oh, shut your mouth!'

They walked happily away. And all around them, people were smiling and kissing their friends and relatives. Love, actually, was all around.

ACTIVITIES

Chapters 1–2

Before you read

1 Have you seen or heard about the film *Love Actually*? What do you know about it? For example, which stars are in it? At what time of the year does the story take place? If you don't know, you will find this information in the Introduction.

2 Look at the Word List at the back of this book. Find four words for jobs.

While you read

3 Write the names of these people.
   a He is an ageing rock star. ....
   b His wife has just died. ....
   c It is her wedding day. ....
   d He is the new Prime Minister. ....
   e She has a new job at 10 Downing Street. ....
   f His girlfriend prefers his brother. ....
   g He has lost his mother. ....
   h He films the wedding. ....
   i She has loved Karl for years. ....
   j He is Billy's manager. ....

After you read

4 Who is speaking? Who or what are they talking about?
   a 'This is rubbish, isn't it?'
   b 'I'm the lobster.'
   c 'How inconvenient.'
   d 'No, no, no is the answer.'
   e 'It would be best for all of us, I think.'
   f 'Has there been a worse song this century?'

5 Work in pairs. Have this conversation.

   Student A: You are the new British Prime Minister. Ask your secretary questions about life at 10 Downing Street. Tell her what you want (for example, how often you will have parties, who you do and do not want to see).

Student B: You are the new British Prime Minister's secretary. Answer his questions. Ask questions about organizing his working life (for example, whether the Prime Minister wants a computer in his living room or drinks in his office).

Chapters 3–4

Before you read

6 Discuss how these characters are probably feeling and why.
the Prime Minister   Jamie   Billy and Joe   Daniel and Sam
Peter and Juliet

While you read

7 Put these events in the order in which they happen in the story. Number them 1–6.
a Jamie arrives in France.   .....
b The Prime Minister learns more about Natalie.   .....
c Sam tells Daniel that he is in love.   .....
d Television viewers complain about Billy.   .....
e Harry finds that he has feelings for Mia.   .....
f Juliet asks for Mark's help.   .....

After you read

8 Whose job is it to:
a bring tea and biscuits to the Prime Minister?
b organize Fairtrade's Christmas party?
c look after Sam?
d run an art gallery?
e clean Jamie's house in France?

9 Discuss these questions. What do you think?
a How does the Prime Minister see Britain's relationship with the US?
b Why does Mark find it so difficult to talk to Juliet?
c What communication problems do Jamie and Aurelia have? How could they communicate better?

Chapters 5–6

Before you read

10 Discuss the person that you are most interested in. What has happened to them? What do you think will happen next?

While you read

11 Are these sentences true (T) or false (F)?

a The US President is a married man.   .....

b The Prime Minister is Karen's uncle.   .....

c Karen's husband runs Fairtrade.   .....

d Jamie is a writer.   .....

e Juliet is in love with Mark.   .....

f Sam loves a girl called Josephine.   .....

g Karl knows Sarah's brother.   .....

h Harry buys his wife a necklace.   .....

After you read

12 Answer the questions.

a How does the Prime Minister's attitude to the US President change? Why?

b Why does Karen feel that her life is not very meaningful?

c Why can't Jamie just print off another copy of his book?

d How does Mark feel while watching the wedding video with Juliet? Why?

e How does Sam plan to win Joanna's heart?

f Why does Sarah always answer her phone when her brother calls?

g Why does Harry become so anxious in the shop?

13 Discuss these statements. How true are they, in your opinion?

a 'I'm not sure politics and women go together.'

b 'If a friend bullies us, he stops being our friend.'

c 'There isn't just one person for each of us.'

d 'Christmas shopping – never an easy or a pleasant job.'

14 Britain is 'a country of Shakespeare, Churchill, the Beatles, Sean Connery, Harry Potter, David Beckham's right foot – and David Beckham's left foot.' Who are, or were, these famous Britons? How would you describe your country, with similar humour?

Chapters 7–9

Before you read

15 Discuss how these people are feeling at this point, and why.

the Prime Minister   Natalie   Harry   Karen   Mia   Jamie
Aurelia   Mark   Juliet   Daniel   Sam   Billy   Karl   Sarah

While you read

16 Complete each sentence.
    a Harry gives Karen a ....
    b Billy's record reaches number .... in the music charts.
    c Jamie gives his family .... and then leaves.
    d Mark uses .... to explain his feelings to Juliet.
    e Billy prefers to be in Joe's .... than Elton John's house.
    f Natalie takes the Prime Minister to a school ....
    g While Joanna sings, Sam plays the ....
    h At the airport, Joanna gives him a ....
    i Jamie asks Aurelia to marry him in a Portuguese ....

After you read

17 At the end of the book, which of these people are arriving in
    Britain? Who is waiting for them? Which people are meeting their
    friends? Who are they meeting?
    Joe   Mark   Harry   Sam   the Prime Minister

18 Work in pairs. Have this conversation.
    Student A: You are a radio DJ. Interview Billy Mack about his
                  successful record and his plans for the future.
    Student B: You are Billy Mack. Answer the DJ's questions.

19 Discuss these questions. Give reasons for your answers.
    a Who has behaved worst in this story? Who has behaved best?
    b Is Karen right to stay with Harry?
    c Was Daniel right to take Sam's feelings for Joanna seriously?
    d Do you think Daniel should tell Carol about his interest in
       Claudia Schiffer?
    e Where should Jamie and Aurelia live? In his country, her country
       or the country where they met?
    f Can a prime minister keep a new girlfriend happy and do his
       job?

Writing

20 Imagine that you are Harry and you are away from home on a business trip. Write to Karen and tell her how sorry you are for hurting her. Tell her why your relationship with her is important to you.

21 Imagine that you are Sam or Joanna (on holiday in the US). Write explaining your feelings, and saying what you have been doing.

22 Write the Prime Minister's report to his ministers, explaining why you have decided that the special relationship between Britain and the US must change. (Don't include Natalie's name!)

23 Write a postcard from Jamie to his brother from France, about Aurelia and the book. Decide whether or not to write about Katya.

24 Write about the Christmas concert for a school newspaper. Say how good it was and thank everybody who helped with it.

25 What did you like about this book? What did you not like? Which story, and which characters, did you like best? Why?

WORD LIST

actually (adv) a word used to say what is really true or surprising

art gallery (n) a room or building where you can look at famous paintings

best man (n) the man who stands next to the man who is getting married, usually his best friend

biscuit (n) a small, thin, dry cake, which is usually sweet

bully (n/v) a person who uses their power to frighten or hurt weaker people

carol (n) a song that people sing at Christmas

charts (n pl) weekly lists of the most popular records

darling (n) a word used when you are talking to someone you love

departure (n) the act of leaving a place, especially at the start of a journey

designer (n) someone whose job is to plan how something is made

DJ (n) someone who introduces popular music on radio or TV, or in clubs

file (n) a collection of papers containing information about a person or subject

funeral (n) an occasion when people say goodbye to someone who has died

honeymoon (n) a holiday that people have after their wedding

lobster (n) a sea animal with eight legs

mistletoe (n) a plant with small, white, round fruit. At Christmas, in Britain, people stand under it and kiss.

naked (adj) not wearing any clothes

necklace (n) jewellery that you wear around your neck

nod (v) to move your head up and down, usually to say yes

plump (adj) slightly fat

Prime Minister (n) the leader of the government in Britain

reception (n) a big formal party to celebrate a marriage

recording studio (n) a room where recordings are made for CDs

rehearsal (n) a time when people practise before a public performance

respect (n) admiration for, or politeness to, an important or skilled person

screen (n) the flat, glass part at the front of a television or a computer

stag night (n) a social occasion when a man goes out with male friends just before his wedding

stepfather (n) a man who is married to your mother, but who is not your father. You are his **stepson**.

trust (v) to believe that a person will not harm you in any way

vicar (n) a person who performs religious duties in the Church of England